The Audit Risk Model

Steven M. Bragg

Table of Contents

About the Author

Steven Bragg, CPA, has been the chief financial officer or controller of four companies, as well as a consulting manager at Ernst & Young. He received a master's degree in finance from Bentley College, an MBA from Babson College, and a Bachelor's degree in Economics from the University of Maine. He has been a two-time president of the Colorado Mountain Club, and is an avid alpine skier, mountain biker, and certified master diver. Mr. Bragg resides in Centennial, Colorado. He has written more than 300 books and courses, including *New Controller Guidebook*, *GAAP Guidebook*, and *Payroll Management*.

Steven maintains the accountingtools.com web site, which contains continuing professional education courses, the Accounting Best Practices podcast, and thousands of articles on accounting subjects.

Buy Additional AccountingTools Courses

AccountingTools offers more than 1,500 hours of CPE courses, with concentrations in accounting, auditing, finance, taxation, and ethics. Related courses that you might like include:

- Guide to Auditor Legal Liability
- How to Conduct an Audit Engagement
- Internal Auditing Guidebook
- The Green Book Explained
- The Yellow Book Explained

Go to accountingtools.com/cpe to view these additional courses.

The Audit Risk Model

Introduction

Audit risk is the risk that an auditor expresses an incorrect opinion when financial statements are materially misstated. Since there are serious negative ramifications associated with an incorrect opinion, it is essential for the auditor to reduce audit risk to an acceptable level. This can be done by brute force, examining every transaction in which a client has engaged. However, such an approach would be far too expensive, so instead the auditor determines the quantity and quality of audit procedures that need to be conducted, based on the audit risk model. In this manual, we describe how the model works, both on a theoretical and practical level, and how the auditor then acts on this information to collect audit evidence.

The Audit Risk Model

The *audit risk model* determines the total amount of risk associated with an audit, and describes how this risk can be managed. The model incorporates three types of audit risk into the following equation:

Audit risk (AR) = Control risk (CR) × Detection risk (DR) × Inherent risk (IR)

Or,

$$AR = CR \times DR \times IR$$

The three types of audit risk included in the equation are expanded upon as follows:

- *Control risk.* This is the risk that potential material misstatements would not be detected or prevented by a client's control systems. When there are significant control failures, a client is more likely to experience undocumented asset losses, which means that its financial statements may reveal a profit when there is actually a loss. In this situation, the auditor cannot rely on the client's control system when devising an audit plan.
- *Detection risk.* This is the risk that the audit procedures used are not capable of detecting a material misstatement. This is especially likely when there are several misstatements that are individually immaterial, but which are material when aggregated. The outcome is that the auditor would conclude that there is no material misstatement of the financial statements when such an error actually exists. Increasing the quantity and especially the quality of audit procedures will reduce detection risk.
- *Inherent risk.* This is the risk that a client's financial statements are susceptible to material misstatements in the absence of any internal controls to guard against such misstatement. Inherent risk is greater when a high degree of judgment is involved in business transactions, since this introduces the risk that

an inexperienced person is more likely to make an error. It is also more likely when significant estimates must be included in transactions, where an estimation error can be made. Inherent risk is also more likely when the transactions in which a client engages are highly complex, and so are more likely to be completed or recorded incorrectly. Finally, this risk is present when a client engages in non-routine transactions for which it has no procedures or controls, thereby making it easier for employees to complete them incorrectly.

Of these three risks, only detection risk is largely under the control of the auditor. That being said, there will always be some amount of detection risk, due to the inherent limitations of an audit. These inherent limitations are caused by the following issues:

- *The nature of the financial reporting.* The creation of financial statements usually involves a certain amount of subjective decision-making, where there is a range of possible numerical values that may be considered acceptable. This means that some line items will inherently be subject to a certain amount of variability that cannot be resolved by adding more audit procedures.
- *The nature of the audit procedures conducted.* There are limitations on an auditor's ability to obtain audit evidence, because the information provided by the client may not be complete, there is always a fraud risk, and the auditor does not have the legal power to conduct a proper investigation into wrongdoing at a client.
- *The timing and cost restrictions imposed on an audit.* The auditor must make sufficient time and resources available to conduct an audit. Nonetheless, it is impracticable to address all information that may exist, or to pursue every matter in exhaustive detail. Consequently, the auditor is expected to focus resources on those areas most likely to contain risks of material misstatement, which means that reduced resources are targeted at other areas of an audit.

The standard approach to the evaluation of risk is to first assess control risk and inherent risk, and use this information to decide upon the most appropriate *planned* level of detection risk. Then, audit programs are designed to obtain the audit evidence that will support the planned level of detection risk. To arrive at the planned level of detection risk, the following modified version of the audit risk equation can be used:

Planned level of detection risk = (Control risk × Inherent risk) ÷ Acceptable audit risk

The concept is expanded upon in the following example.

EXAMPLE

An auditor is conducting an initial assessment of a new client, where the acceptable audit risk is 5%. The control risk is initially assessed to be 50%, while the inherent risk is assessed at 90%. By plugging this information into the revised audit risk equation, he arrives at the following outcome:

Planned level of detection risk = (0.50 control risk × 0.90 Inherent risk) ÷ 0.05 acceptable audit risk

Planned level of detection risk = 9%

Given these risk levels, the auditor needs to plan his substantive audit tests to reduce the risk of not detecting material misstatements to 9%.

Though this model seems simple enough, the problem is how to derive the inputs to the model. It is not possible to quantify any of the inputs to the planned level of detection risk – which means that the 9% planned level of detection risk noted in the preceding example could have been half that amount or double it simply by changing an estimate. Another concern is that, since every input to the equation is subjective, how can we realistically expect to multiply and divide them? In essence, we are attempting to apply mathematical concepts to opinions. Nonetheless, the equation is a useful way to conceptualize how an audit program should be constructed to collect a sufficient amount of appropriate audit evidence.

Given the subjectivity of the various components of audit risk, auditors typically assign a high, medium, or low risk to each one. Or, the auditor may assign a high, medium, or low risk assessment to a combination of control risk and inherent risk. In either case, a high, medium, or low risk assessment for *control* risk or *inherent* risk corresponds to a high, medium, or low *audit* risk.

How do auditors come up with these high, medium, or low risk assessments? Let's start with inherent risk. As noted in our earlier definition of inherent risk, it tends to be higher in more complex environments where judgments, estimates, and non-routine transactions are common. In these situations, a high risk is likely to be assigned. In practice, the conservative auditor is more likely to assign a high inherent risk in the majority of audit engagements. The assignment of a rating to control risk will depend on the outcome of the auditor's testing of client internal controls (see the Types of Audit Tests section later in this manual). Minimal numbers of control exceptions will justify a low risk rating, which increasing numbers of exceptions should correspond to either a medium or high risk rating.

Outcomes of Risk Combinations

Since we have just pointed out that high, medium, and low risk classifications are usually assigned to the various sub-categories of audit risk, this brings up the question of which combinations of these risks result in acceptable and unacceptable audit risk.

In nearly all audit engagements, audit risk must be low. To achieve this, one should be mindful of the risk outcomes described in the following tables, where we present every possible combination of high, medium, and low risk levels for all three types of risk.

<u>Risk Levels Cause Unacceptable Audit Risk</u> (in all of the following risk combinations, every risk level is either medium or high; the typical outcome would be a disclaimer or a qualified opinion)

Control Risk	Detection Risk	Inherent Risk	Commentary
High	High	High	When management does not maintain an acceptable system of internal control, is not interested in maintaining adequate accounting records, and sources of reliable evidence appear to be inadequate.
High	High	Medium	The presence of a high control risk calls for a substantial increase in substantive audit procedures; when the detection risk is also high, then the cost of those procedures will be too high to make the engagement cost-effective.
High	Medium	High	Same as the first condition, where a moderate level of detection risk is not sufficient to offset the other two high risks.
High	Medium	Medium	Same as the medium | medium | medium set of risk conditions listed at the bottom of this table.
Medium	High	High	Same as the first condition, but management does not maintain all aspects of internal controls at an acceptable level.
Medium	High	Medium	In this case, the medium level of control risk and inherent risk will call for a substantial amount of substantive audit procedures to offset; if the detection risk is also high, then the cost of those procedures will be too high to make the engagement cost-effective.
Medium	Medium	High	Where the client environment is highly complex, resulting in high inherent risk. This risk is not adequately offset, since the auditor still has limited concerns about control risk and detection risk.
Medium	Medium	Medium	Given the across-the-board medium risk ratings, the audit procedures needed to achieve a low detection risk would not be cost-effective.

EXAMPLE

Bugaboo Consulting operates 375 process consulting offices in 50 countries. Each office manager has the power to set prices, issue billings, and handle incoming and outgoing cash transactions. Control systems are unique to each office. Furthermore, each office records transactions in its own accounting system using local account definitions and a unique chart of accounts to develop a set of financial statements that are in a non-standard format.

In this situation, the auditors consider control risk to be high. In addition, because of travel costs, it is not cost-effective to travel to a reasonable number of the locations to conduct substantive tests, resulting in a high detection risk. Finally, given the complexity of the operating environment, the inherent risk is also judged to be high. Given the high across-the-board risk level, the audit risk will be so high that the auditor should disclaim an opinion.

<u>Risk Levels Allow for Possible Acceptable Audit Risk</u> (in all of the following risk combinations, there is a possible outcome that could lead the auditor to conclude that an acceptable audit risk exists)

Control Risk	Detection Risk	Inherent Risk	Commentary
High	Low	High	This situation exists when the cost of the audit procedures needed to offset the high control risk and inherent risk are relatively low.
High	Low	Medium	A very low detection risk may be needed to offset the high control risk, which could be difficult for the auditor to achieve.
High	High	Low	It would be very difficult to achieve a reasonable audit risk in this situation; only a very low inherent risk would make this risk combination tenable.
High	Medium	Low	The high control risk and low inherent risk may offset each other, leaving detection risk as the key variable for the auditor to focus on.
Medium	Low	High	In this case, the combination of medium control risk and low detection risk would probably result in a judgment that audit risk is acceptable.
Medium	Low	Medium	The low detection risk makes it possible to offset the other two conditions when they are at the medium level.
Medium	High	Low	Same as the immediately preceding set of risks, except that the improved inherent risk situation makes it more likely that a reasonable audit risk can be achieved.
Medium	Medium	Low	Achieving an acceptable audit risk is fairly likely, given the absence of any high risks.
Low	High	High	The controlling factor here is a high degree of client complexity that leads to a high inherent risk, probably combined with high testing costs that make it difficult to reduce the detection risk. Control risk is not a factor.
Low	Medium	High	Same as the preceding condition, though detection risk is reduced somewhat.
Low	High	Medium	The low control risk offsets the medium inherent risk, so the variable becomes the cost of the procedures needed to drive down the detection risk.
Low	Medium	Medium	Same as the immediately preceding set of risks, though the cost of driving down the detection risk is likely to be reduced.
Low	High	Low	Any combination of two low risks will yield an acceptable audit risk.

EXAMPLE

A company operates a home repair operation, where inventory items (such as compressors for refrigerators) are high-value. Service technicians check out inventory items and assign them to jobs. The high value of the inventory leads the auditor to assign a high inherent risk to the engagement. The control risk is assessed as minimal, since the control system is well-designed, was properly implemented, and is functioning correctly. It will be necessary for the auditor to conduct substantive tests, but the cost that will be incurred to drive down detection risk will be quite high.

In this case, it is up to the auditor to decide whether the low control risk adequately offsets the other two risks to the extent that the resulting audit risk is acceptable.

<u>Risk Levels Will Result in Acceptable Audit Risk</u> (in all of the following risk combinations, at least two of the risks are rated as being low)

Control Risk	Detection Risk	Inherent Risk	Commentary
High	Low	Low	Any combination of two low risks will yield an acceptable audit risk.
Medium	Low	Low	Any combination of two low risks will yield an acceptable audit risk.
Low	Low	High	Any combination of two low risks will yield an acceptable audit risk.
Low	Low	Medium	Any combination of two low risks will yield an acceptable audit risk.
Low	Medium	Low	Any combination of two low risks will yield an acceptable audit risk.
Low	Low	Low	Any combination of two low risks will yield an acceptable audit risk.

When planning an audit engagement, the auditor must review each of the subsidiary levels of risk to determine the total amount of audit risk. If the risk level is too high, the auditor conducts additional procedures to reduce the risk to an acceptable level. The following key points relate to the audit risk model:

- *Impact of control risk changes.* When the expected effectiveness of the control system is low, then the level of assurance provided by other audit procedures must be increased; this means that the auditor must engage in a significantly increased amount of tests of details or substantive tests. When the control system is considered to be effective, then the use of other audit procedures can be decreased.
- *When to increase the sample size.* When the level of control risk and inherent risk is high, the auditor can increase the sample size for audit testing, thereby reducing detection risk.

- *When to decrease the sample size.* When control risk and inherent risk are considered to be low, it is safer for the auditor to reduce the sample size for audit testing, though doing so increases detection risk.

> **Tip:** Auditor knowledge of a client's control risk may span several years, going back to the results of prior audits, so be sure to consult prior year working papers when estimating control risk.

The Reasonable Assurance Requirement

Once the auditor has delved into the audit risk model and evaluated the amount of control, detection, and inherent risk, there are two decisions to make. The first is whether it is even possible to begin (or continue) the audit, given the discovery of high risk levels; the first of the preceding tables addresses these scenarios. If the auditor decides to proceed, then it will be necessary to obtain reasonable assurance that the client's financial statements are free of material misstatements. A reasonable level of assurance is considered to be a high level of assurance, though not an absolute one. To achieve reasonable assurance, the auditor needs to obtain sufficient appropriate audit evidence to reduce audit risk to an acceptably low level. We discuss audit evidence next.

The Nature of Audit Evidence

Audit evidence is any information used by the auditor to arrive at the conclusions upon which an auditor's opinion is based. Audit evidence may be contained within the accounting records of a client, or it may be obtained elsewhere. Accounting records are the initial accounting entries and supporting records of a client, such as invoices, checks, contracts, journal entries, and ledgers, as well as spreadsheets, computations, and reconciliations. Audit evidence is obtained through a variety of activities, including inquiries, confirmations, inspections, observations, recalculations, and analytical procedures.

Alternative sources of audit evidence (that is, *not* from a client's accounting records) include the following:

- Previous audits
- The work of management's or auditor's specialists
- The work of the client's internal auditors or their efforts on behalf of the auditor

Audit evidence may also be obtained from the absence of information. For example, the refusal of management to provide certain kinds of information constitutes a form of audit evidence.

Two aspects of audit evidence are its sufficiency and its appropriateness. The *sufficiency* concept relates to the quantity of audit evidence collected. Sufficiency is critical when there is a higher assessed level of material misstatement. The *appropriateness* concept relates to the quality of the evidence collected. The two aspects are interrelated, since a high level of appropriateness may allow the auditor to collect a smaller quantity of evidence (and vice versa). However, this concept does not always work, since obtaining more audit evidence does not necessarily compensate for a poor level of appropriateness.

The amount of audit evidence needed to support the auditor's opinion is cumulative in nature, so the amount of additional evidence compiled as an auditor proceeds is, in some part, derived from the results already obtained. The auditor's goal is to obtain sufficient appropriate audit evidence to reduce the level of audit risk to an acceptably low level.

Sources of Audit Evidence

Audit evidence may be derived in a number of ways, as noted in the following subsections.

Testing

One approach is to test the accounting records. There are many ways to test the records, such as by reperforming procedures and reconciling account balances. However, even if testing reveals that a client's accounting records are internally consistent and roll up correctly into the financial statements, this does not provide sufficient appropriate audit evidence to form an opinion on the client's financial statements.

Inspection

Another source of audit evidence is inspection, which involves the examination of a client's records or the physical inspection of its assets. For example, the auditor could inspect purchase orders for evidence of authorization, or inspect checks for evidence that they were appropriately signed. Or, the inspection of a sales contract could lead the auditor to conclusions about how the client should be recognizing the revenue associated with the contract. Perhaps the most common of all inspection activities is the auditor's participation in a client's physical inventory count process, where the auditor may review individual inventory items to verify their existence.

Observation

Yet another source of audit evidence is the use of observation, which involves looking at a process that is being performed by client personnel. For example, the auditor could observe how a client's warehouse team conducts the year-end inventory count. However, there are several weaknesses in the observation concept; one is that being observed may alter the behavior of the persons carrying out a process, while another concern is that observations only deal with a specific point in time – the process being reviewed could change substantially at other times of the year.

Confirmation

A high-quality source of audit evidence is the external confirmation. These are direct written responses to the auditor by an outside party, confirming such matters as receivable, payable, bank account, and loan balances. Confirmations are a highly-reliable form of audit evidence, since they are obtained from independent sources, and are more reliable than evidence that is obtained indirectly or by inference. The use of confirmations can be especially useful in obtaining audit evidence with a high degree of reliability, which may be needed when the auditor is responding to significant risks of material misstatement.

Though confirmations usually only deal with ending balances, the auditor can expand these requests to include the terms of agreements, or of any changes to those agreements.

The auditor is required to use confirmation procedures for accounts receivable, unless the overall account balance is immaterial, doing so would be ineffective, or the assessed material misstatement risk is low and other planned procedures will address the assessed risk.

Recalculation

The auditor may choose to check the mathematical accuracy of a client's records.

Reperformance

The auditor can elect to independently execute the procedures or controls associated with a targeted activity that had already been performed as part of the client's system of internal controls.

Analytical Procedures

The auditor can engage in a series of evaluations of a client's financial information by comparing the relationships between various financial and operational information, such as sales per person or a historical trend analysis of the gross margin percentage. The intent is to identify fluctuations in these outcomes that are inconsistent with other relevant information, or that differ from expectations. This approach can also involve the use of benchmarking data, to see if a client's financial results and financial position are reasonable when compared to similar information for competitors.

Scanning

A variation on analytical procedures is for the auditor to scan client data to identify significant or unusual items to examine further, such as by examining unusual journal entries, general ledger balances, adjusting entries, suspense accounts, reconciliations, and so forth. The use of electronic scanning can be used to examine entire populations of client data for these anomalies. The results of these examinations constitute additional audit evidence. This approach also results in additional evidence, in that the auditor has exercised professional judgment in determining that the items not selected for further analysis are less likely to be misstated.

Inquiry

A mainstay activity is for the auditor to gather audit evidence through ongoing inquiries. The most effective inquiries result from discussions with knowledgeable persons, both within and outside of the client entity, on the full range of audit topics being examined. Inquiries can cover a broad range of topics, such as asking whether there have been any cases in which management has overridden company controls, or whether there are any additional lease arrangements that do not appear in the financial statements. These results may lead the auditor to construct additional audit procedures to investigate topics that had not initially been main targets of the audit.

Inquiries can also be useful for background information, such as understanding management's reasons for taking certain actions, or why it chose to stop pursuing certain activities.

Evidence Obtained from the Work of Others

The auditor may choose to use the work of a client's internal audit function to obtain audit evidence, or use internal auditors to provide direct assistance to the engagement team. The extent to which internal audit personnel or their work can be used depends on their level of objectivity and competence, as well as whether they apply a systematic and disciplined approach to the conduct of their work. Incorporating a client's internal audit staff and its work into an audit can reduce the extent of the work performed by the auditor, but it does not reduce the auditor's responsibility for the audit opinion expressed.

The auditor may make use of the work of an individual or organization that has expertise in an area other than accounting or auditing. Examples of areas in which an auditor may choose to use the work of a specialist are:

- Actuarial calculations of benefit plan liabilities
- Estimates of environmental liabilities
- Estimates of oil and gas reserves
- Interpretations of complex tax compliance issues
- Interpretations of laws and regulations
- The valuation of financial instruments and nonfinancial assets measured at fair value

Making use of the work of an auditor's specialist can result in valid audit evidence, but the auditor is still solely responsible for the audit opinion expressed, not the specialist.

The extent to which the auditor elects to use the work of an auditor's specialist will depend on the following issues:

- The nature of the work to be conducted.
- The risks of material misstatements associated with the work to be conducted.
- The significance of the work to be performed in relation to the audit.

- The auditor's knowledge of the specialist's prior work.
- Whether the specialist will be subject to the auditor's quality control procedures.

The auditor also needs to consider the competence and capability of a specialist, since these issues can impact whether the work of the specialist will be adequate for the auditor's purposes.

Audit Sampling

The massive amounts of data generated by audit clients make it quite difficult for auditors to examine 100% of all records, unless data analytics tools[1] are used. For the many cases to which data analytics cannot be applied, the most efficient alternative is audit sampling. *Audit sampling* is the use of an audit procedure to select and evaluate less than 100% of a population, where the items selected are expected to be representative of the population, and which can therefore provide a reasonable basis for conclusions about the population.

The goal of audit sampling is to arrive at a subset of selections from a population that is representative of the entire population being sampled. By being representative, the results obtained from the sample should correspond to the results that would otherwise have been obtained by examining every item in the targeted population. This does not mean that the projected misstatement resulting from a statistically-derived sample will exactly match the misstatement in an entire population, only that the selected sample will be representative of the population.

Procedures Not Involving Audit Sampling

There are a number of audit procedures that do *not* involve the use of audit sampling. These procedures fall into the following general classifications:

- *Analytical procedures.* These procedures involve the analysis of comparisons between financial and nonfinancial data, as well as the identification of fluctuations that differ from expectations. These comparisons and analyses are based on aggregated amounts of data, and so do not involve sampling.[2]
- *Automated IT control tests.* When testing the functionality of automated controls, a single test of each automated control may be adequate for placing reliance on each control.
- *Full population analysis.* There are situations in which the auditor elects to examine every item within a population, or every item within a subset of that population (such as every fixed asset purchase exceeding $10,000). Since 100% of the population is under review, this cannot be considered sampling.
- *Inquiries and observations.* Auditors routinely make inquiries and observe client operations. For example, they may conduct interviews with client

---

[1] See the author's *Guide to Data Analytics for Audits* manual for more information.
[2] See the author's *Guide to Analytical Procedures* manual for more information.

employees, observe the operation of controls, and observe the presence of fixed assets.
- *Selected tests of controls.* Some tests of controls are not based on sampling. Examples are tests of automated application controls, the segregation of duties, and when the performance of a control is not documented.

It may be useful to clarify the nature of sampling and nonsampling audit activities with an example. An audit client has purchased an additional $10 million of fixed assets during the past year, of which the top 10 assets acquired constitute $7.5 million of the total amount of acquisitions, while 200 other assets make up the remaining $2.5 million of purchases. It would be reasonable for the auditor to examine all of the top 10 assets, and then apply audit sampling to the other 200 assets. By doing so, the auditor is reducing the risk of material misstatement from the full $10 million to just $2.5 million of the total. Despite this obvious approach, the auditor actually has several options for how to deal with the residual $2.5 million of asset purchases, which are noted in the following exhibit.

Sampling and Nonsampling Alternatives

Nonsampling Approach #1	Nonsampling Approach #2	Sampling Approach
Based on a low level of assessed control risk for the $2.5 million of purchases, the auditor chooses to scan the fixed asset entries for unusual items, and then uses analytical procedures to assess the probability of a material misstatement.	The auditor concludes that any possible misstatement of the 200 applicable assets would be immaterial. Also, a physical count of the assets was made, which proves their existence but not their valuation. In this situation, the auditor can elect not to conduct any additional procedures.	Assume the same audit activities as Approach #1, but the auditor decides to gather additional evidence with audit sampling.

Statistical vs. Nonstatistical Sampling

Statistics-based audit sampling is derived from the field of applied statistics, and requires some degree of training to use properly. Conversely, nonstatistical methods are derived from the auditor's expertise, both in making selections from a population and in evaluating the results. Another difference is the use of a more formal testing structure for statistical sampling, which includes the numerical evaluation of sampling outcomes. Conversely, a nonstatistical sample is usually selected in a manner that makes the auditor believe that it will be representative of the population. There is no requirement to compute a sample size using statistical theory when calculating the sample size for a nonstatistical sampling application; instead, the auditor relies on professional judgment and a knowledge of statistical concepts.

It is a matter of professional judgment for the auditor in deciding whether to use a statistical or nonstatistical sampling approach. One who elects to use nonstatistical sampling must use professional judgment in determining the appropriate sample size. Usually, the sample size selected would be roughly comparable to the sample size selected for a statistically-derived sample.

> **Note:** Both the use of statistical and nonstatistical methods comply with auditing standards.

The Audit Sampling Process

When engaged in audit sampling, the auditor's intent is to corroborate the accuracy of targeted client data, usually in regard to certain types of transactions, the detail comprising an account balance, or to evaluate the effectiveness of client controls. The intent is to evaluate whether an amount is materially misstated.

A unique characteristic of the accounting data being sampled is that it tends to include a small number of quite large items and a large number of small items. This distribution can lead the auditor to stratify the population, with all larger items being examined in detail, while using sampling to investigate the smaller items.

No matter how much sampling is used, the auditor will rarely rely on just the results of the sampling when forming an audit opinion. Instead, a number of interrelated tests will be performed, with the results of all procedures being used to develop an opinion. This means that the auditor will plan his or her audit sampling procedures knowing that other supplementary procedures will also be used.

Audit Sample Assessment

When reviewing sampled items, the auditor must develop an assessment of them. Possible options are:

- Treat the item as a deviation or misstatement if it cannot be found.
- Project the results of the sample to the population from which the item was taken, even if the client corrects any deviations or misstatements found.
- Compare the projected deviation rate or misstatement to the tolerable level for the test.
- Consider the qualitative aspects of the deviation or misstatement to see if there are other issues, such as fraud, that need to be addressed in the audit.

Types of Audit Tests

An audit may encompass several types of audit tests, each having a somewhat different purpose. The testing choices are as follows:

- *Tests of controls*. These procedures test the effectiveness of a control in preventing or detecting a material misstatement. Depending on the results of this test, the auditor may choose to rely upon a client's system of controls as part of the audit plan. However, if the test reveals that controls are weak, the auditor will enhance the use of substantive testing (see next), which typically increases the cost of the audit. A test of controls is made, irrespective of the dollar amount of the underlying business transaction; the main point of the test is to see if a control functions properly, so the dollar amount of a transaction is not of consequence to the goal of the test. The following are general classifications of tests of controls:

- o *Reperformance.* Initiate a new transaction, to see which controls are used by the client, as well as the effectiveness of those controls.
- o *Observation.* Observe a business process in action, and in particular the control elements of the process.
- o *Inspection.* Examine business documents for approval signatures, stamps, or review check marks, which indicate that controls have been performed. This test is usually conducted for a sample of documents that occurred throughout the year, which provides evidence that the system of controls has operated in a reliable manner throughout the reporting period.

- *Substantive procedures.* These procedures are intended to create evidence to support the assertion that there are no material misstatements in regard to the completeness, validity, and accuracy of a client's financial statements. The procedures include the following categories of activity:

  - o Testing classes of transactions, account balances, and disclosures.
  - o Agreeing the financial statements and accompanying notes to the underlying accounting records.
  - o Examining material journal entries and other adjustments made during the preparation of the financial statements.

- *Dual-purpose tests.* These procedures are used as both a test of controls and a substantive test. They improve the efficiency of an audit, since two tests are being combined into one procedure, where separate procedures are applied to a common sample of transactions. This approach includes a preliminary judgment that there is an acceptably low level of control risk, since the test of controls does not precede any substantive tests. The calculated sample size for this type of test is typically the larger of the samples that would have been designed for two tests if they had been conducted individually.

Risk

The uncertainties related to audit risk encompass the topic of audit sampling, where there is sampling risk and nonsampling risk. They are as follows:

- *Sampling risk.* This is the possibility that the items selected in a sample are not truly representative of the population being tested. It comes from the possibility that a sample selection might contain proportionately more or less of a misstatement or deviation than exists in the population as a whole. This risk includes a conclusion that controls are more or less effective than is really the case, as well as an incorrect acceptance or incorrect rejection for a substantive procedure.

- *Nonsampling risk.* This is the risk of reaching an erroneous conclusion for any reason other than something related to sampling risk. Or, stated differently, nonsampling risk is the probability of arriving at an incorrect conclusion, despite having selected a correct sample. Examples of nonsampling risks are applying inappropriate audit procedures (such as relying on receivable confirmations to reveal the existence of unrecorded receivables), failing to detect a material misstatement, and misinterpreting the results of an audit test. Under these circumstances, even 100% testing of an entire population would not be effective.

When the auditor has a choice of auditing procedures, both of which provide the same level of assurance and at the same approximate cost, one would typically select the procedure having the lower nonsampling risk.

Procedural Planning

Any type of audit sampling involves a significant amount of judgment in planning and performing a procedure, as well as in evaluating its results. As part of the planning process, the auditor can choose to employ either statistical or nonstatistical sampling. Statistical sampling is more likely to yield an efficient sample, and allow for the determination of how sufficient the resulting sample is, *and* yield a quantitative evaluation of the results. If a sampling procedure does not allow for the numerical measurement of sampling risk, then it is considered a nonstatistical sampling procedure. This does not mean that a properly designed nonstatistical sampling procedure cannot provide equally effective results, only that it cannot explicitly measure sampling risk.

The auditor will require training in order to properly apply statistical sampling. However, this training can be significantly reduced by using audit sampling software, which can greatly simplify the task of selecting samples. Unfortunately, this software is most applicable to situations in which the population is already in an electronic format. When this is not the case, the auditor may need to conduct a manual selection.

EXAMPLE

An auditor is conducting the year-end physical inventory count for Slobbering Dog Brewery. The auditor wants to apply statistical sampling to test the physical inventory count. Unfortunately, Slobbering Dog only maintains a periodic inventory system, so there are no detailed quantity listings to sample. In this case, the auditor will likely need to use a nonstatistical sampling approach.

There are several issues for the auditor to consider when developing an audit sampling procedure. These considerations are as follows:

1. Determine the account balance or class of transactions to be examined. The auditor will normally identify items within a population that are individually of interest, such as unusually high-value inventory items during a physical count, or a large credit memo as part of a review of accounts receivable. This

    determination should be based on the auditor's knowledge of the items under review. For example, the auditor may know that certain inventory items are subject to obsolescence, and so will tag them for review. In other cases, the auditor may believe that a 100% examination of the population is more efficient, or because he does not want to incur any sampling risk. The items identified during this stage may be fully examined.

2. Completion of the first step will leave a residual group that the auditor needs to evaluate in order to reach the audit objective. For example, this may involve using audit sampling for the remaining balance in an account, after all large-value items have been examined.

Sampling Plans

There are several types of sampling plans that an auditor can consider when engaging in audit sampling. The first of these plans is *attribute sampling*, which involves the selection of a small number of transactions and making assumptions about how their characteristics represent the full population of which the selected items are a part. The concept is used to test a population for certain characteristics, such as the presence of an authorizing signature or approval stamp on a document. The concept can be used to determine whether various accounting controls are functioning in a reliable manner. The result of attribute sampling is binary – either a condition exists or it does not exist. Thus, there is no gray area in attribute sampling. Also, equal weight is given to each occurrence or deviation from a control, no matter what the dollar amount of each transaction may be. Attribute sampling is commonly applied to the systems of controls associated with payables, billings, and payroll. Examples of typical attribute sampling tests are:

- 50 out of 60 invoices were supported by a sales order.
- 38 out of 40 supplier invoices that were greater than $1,000 contained an approval signature.
- 19 out of 20 fixed asset purchases had a supporting authorization document signed by the company president.
- Three out of 80 invoices are overdue for payment.
- The early payment discount was not taken on two out of 11 supplier invoices.
- 13 out of 211 journal entries were posted to the wrong account.

The results of an attribute sampling test are then compared to the tolerable error rate established for that test. If the test results are worse than the tolerable error rate, the control point related to the test has failed, and should be revised or replaced. When the tested sampling rate falls just outside the acceptable error rate, it is possible that conducting more tests with a larger sample size will result in an actual error rate that falls within the acceptable error rate. Thus, the first reaction to a marginal attribute sampling result is to keep on testing with a larger sample group. This expansion of the sample size frequently does not yield a better result, as the original smaller sample size already provided the correct insight into the underlying error rate.

Another type of sampling plan is *variables sampling*, which is the process used to predict the value of a specific variable within a population. In auditing, this means calculating the dollar value of an account balance or determining whether an account is materially misstated. It is mostly used to determine the reasonableness of recorded amounts. Variables sampling is typically used to test the accuracy of inventory quantities, receivables, payroll expense, and additions to fixed assets. These outcomes include a statistical derivation of the plus or minus range of the total receivables value that is under review.

A third type of sampling plan relates to the connections between sampling of the balance sheet and income statement. It is quite common for sampling of the balance sheet to allow the auditor to draw conclusions about income statement accounts. For example, the confirmation of accounts receivable and tests of cash collections will also provide some assurance to the auditor regarding the revenue accounts in the income statement. The nature of these interrelationships can be considered when deciding whether additional audit evidence is needed in relation to income statement accounts. There will, however, be instances in which the sampling of balance sheet accounts will not provide sufficient assurances regarding income statement accounts. For example, the sales arrangements with certain customers may raise the suspicion that the revenue related to these contracts should be deferred to a later period; if so, separate testing will be needed for these transactions. In short, one must consider the specific circumstances of the client when deciding how (or whether) balance sheet sampling needs to be supplemented in order to address assertions pertaining to the income statement.

The Audit Plan

The initial assessment of audit risk for a client is documented in the associated *audit plan*, which states the overall strategy and detailed steps to be followed in the conduct of an audit. As an audit progresses, the auditor will gradually learn more about the risks associated with the engagement. As this information is collected, it is used to adjust the audit plan, so that the activities the auditor eventually engages in turn out to be somewhat different from those originally stated in the plan. It is possible that the ongoing updates to the plan eventually show that the risks are so high and the lack of evidence so great that it is impossible to complete the engagement.

Summary

The audit risk model is all about identifying the type and severity of the risks associated with an audit engagement. The auditor uses this information to decide whether it is even possible to proceed with an engagement. If so, the next question is how to mitigate each risk type – usually by expanding the quantity and quality of audit evidence. This is a highly judgmental process, which the auditor must constantly review over the course of an engagement as various audit procedures are completed.

Glossary

A

Appropriateness. The quality of audit evidence collected.

Attribute sampling. The selection of a small number of transactions and making assumptions about how their characteristics represent the full population of which the selected items are a part.

Audit evidence. Any information used by the auditor to arrive at the conclusions upon which an auditor's opinion is based.

Audit plan. A statement of the overall strategy and detailed steps to be followed in the conduct of an audit.

Audit risk. The possibility that an auditor's findings or recommendations may be improper, due to incomplete evidence, an inadequate audit process, misleading information, or intentional omissions.

Audit risk model. The equation stating that control risk times detection risk times inherent risk equals audit risk.

Audit sampling. The use of an audit procedure to select and evaluate less than 100% of a population, where the items selected are expected to be representative of the population.

C

Control risk. The risk that potential material misstatements would not be detected or prevented by a client's control systems.

D

Detection risk. The risk that the audit procedures used are not capable of detecting a material misstatement.

Dual-purpose test. A procedure that is used as both a test of controls and a substantive test.

I

Inherent risk. The risk that a client's financial statements are susceptible to material misstatements in the absence of any internal controls to guard against such misstatement.

N

Nonsampling risk. The risk of reaching an erroneous conclusion for any reason other than something related to sampling risk.

S

Sampling risk. The possibility that the items selected in a sample are not truly representative of the population being tested.

Substantive procedure. A procedure intended to create evidence to support the assertion that there are no material misstatements in regard to the completeness, validity, and accuracy of a client's financial statements.

Sufficiency. The quantity of audit evidence collected.

T

Tests of controls. Procedures intended to test the effectiveness of a control in preventing or detecting a material misstatement.

V

Variables sampling. The process used to predict the value of a specific variable within a population.

Index